Diego Rivera

A Selective Annotated Bibliography of

Dissertations and Theses

Louis V. Allene

Allene, Louis V.

Diego Rivera: A selective annotated bibliography of dissertations and theses/Louis V. Allene

p. cm.

1. Rivera, Diego, 1886-1957 -- Criticism and Interpretation. 2. Magic Realism. I. Title.

ND 259 .R5

759

ISBN-10 1511780533

ISBN-13 978-1511780537

Cover – Detroit Industry Mural, North Wall, Diego Rivera

Other titles by Louis V. Allene

Juan Rulfo: A selective annotated bibliography of dissertations and theses

Octavio Paz: A selective annotated bibliography of dissertations and theses

Gabriel Garcia Marquez: A selective annotated bibliography of dissertations and theses

Carlos Fuentes: A selective annotated bibliography of dissertations and theses

Jorge Luis Borges: A selective annotated bibliography of dissertations and theses

Isabel Allende A selective annotated bibliography of dissertations and theses

Jose Donoso: A selective annotated bibliography of dissertations and theses

Frida Kahlo A selective annotated bibliography of dissertations and theses

Diego Rivera: A selective annotated bibliography of dissertations and theses

Magic Realism: A selective annotated bibliography of dissertations and theses

Table of Contents

1.)   **Amaro, F. S.**

Mexican Mural Movement: Myths and mythmakers.

Ph.D. dissertation, Lunds University (Sweden). 2004.

The aim of this study of the Mexican Mural Movement is to analyze the myths it expressed and the myths it produced. The two main characters of my study are the minister José Vasconcelos and the painter Diego Rivera, because I believe these two personalities are indispensable for an understanding of the myths surrounding the Mexican Mural Movement. While the painter is well known, the personality and work of José Vasconcelos has not received the recognition they deserve. I try to analyze and comprehend the context in which the movement began and to find explanations for the generalizations and myths associated with Mexican Muralism. The myths about Mexican Muralism are articulated at diverse levels. Many commentators equate Muralism directly with the Mexican Revolution. In this vision Mexican Mural Movement was a result and, at the same time, a kind of mirror of the Mexican Revolution of 1910, that it was essentially a social-realist art, epic and didactic, that had the historical and revolutionary past as background. Another idea, frequently expressed, is that of the ideological continuity between the pre-Hispanic past and the Mexican Revolution. In my research to understand Mexican mythology as it appeared in the murals and to identify the structural logic and the instrumental aspects of those myths, I came to the conclusion that the mythological idea of Mexico was built and developed in the sub-conscious of Mexicans over the centuries after the conquest. Starting from 1921, it became visible in the painted walls, which helped to form a sort of collective memory. This construction or visual myth, the painted Mexicanidad, functions as a rationalization of the problems and traumas deriving from the process of the Conquest, since all kinds of problems and conflicts seems to be solved in the murals, which also provide hope of a rebirth for the martyred Mexican race.

Rivera's Muralism shows a people and a Revolution that never existed. He promoted representations of a utopian reality, very different from the reality existing away from the walls. However, resistant to all attempts at deconstruction, the murals are there and with their existence testify to another kind of "truth." There exists a perception about Mexican Muralism, more or less widespread, in which Mexico and Mexican Muralism are populated entirely by heroes and villains, and this perception in turn increases the myths about it. This perception is largely based on popular culture, in the mass media and in particular in North American movies, as in the case of the recent film Frida. [Author Abstract]

2.)   **Arellano, C.**

The importance of the xoloitzcuintli in Mexican history and in the works of Diego Rivera and Frida Kahlo.

M.A. thesis, California State University, Los Angeles. 2012.

The image of the Mexican hairless dog, or xoloitzcuintli, has famously been immortalized in Diego Rivera's murals and in the paintings of Frida Kahlo. The xoloitzcuintli has become part of a rich Mexican history. The purpose of this study is to place the dog in Mexican history, trace it back before the Spanish colonization, and reevaluate the role of the xoloitzcuintli in the

Aztec civilization. This would be done in order to understand the impact that this animal had in its society and why it motivated 20th century artists to depict it in their works. [Author Abstract]

3.)   **Beer, M. M.**

Modern Mexican art and history: The art of Diego Rivera and Frida Kahlo.

M.A. thesis, California State University, Dominguez Hills. 1994.

The research contained herein is the result of searching local and university libraries for formerly published research, and will thoroughly examine and discuss particular art works by both Diego Rivera and Frida Kahlo. In addition to the detailed analysis of their respective workmanship, the relevant history and culture of the time period in which they lived will be documented and clarified. Likewise, the societal impact and importance of their specific works will also be studied. Furthermore, the influence of their craft will be considered. The cultural, social and historical forces that brought about their masterpieces will be discussed including the dominant role that politics played in shaping their distinctive works. Finally, the personal significance of their creations will be determined for each artist respectively. [Author Abstract]

4.)   **Castillo, M. A.**

Avant-Garde and Socialist Dreamworlds in Latin America: Global and Local Designs, 1919--1939.

Ph.D. dissertation, Columbia University.

2013.

This dissertation examines the avant-garde as one of the last significant cultural manifestations in Latin America that attempted to offer an alternative to capitalism in the twentieth century. My study redefines the avant-garde as a global critique of modernity whose emergence can only be explained from a geopolitical perspective. During this time, the world order dictated that metropolitan areas like Western Europe be engaged in a mutual economic dependence with peripheral regions such as Latin America. Consequently, a revolutionary socialist impulse originated from within secondary economic areas in the world like Russia and Latin America. Movements such as Dada and Cubism conveyed the necessity for art to break from the autonomous status attributed to it by the bourgeoisie; but ultimately, these aesthetic projects did not address an essential component of the changing social picture, namely the articulation of collective fantasies directed at the emerging masses. The avant-garde was able to articulate these dreamworlds only after art intersected with socialism. With this convergence art claimed a different kind of autonomy, one not based on innocuous insularity but on a socially conscious critical capacity. The revolutionary discourse that resulted from the combination of political and artistic realms aimed at addressing the masses as an integral part of a new modern society. The chapters include muralism (Diego Rivera), periodicals (Amauta), and poetry (César Vallejo). Building upon local and global geopolitical perspectives, these works constructed socialist dreamworlds, expressions of utopian desires to transform the world, against the backdrop of art's tendency toward new modes of production and aesthetic sensibilities in the early twentieth century. Sifting through the ruins of these cultural artifacts, I discuss topics such as the figure of the intellectual and the history of radical ideas in Latin America; Marxism; public art and state sponsorship; iconography of revolution and spectrality; and the autonomy of art at the intersection of politics and aesthetics. [Author Abstract]

5.) **Indych, A. P.**

Mexican muralism without walls: The critical reception of portable work by Orozco, Rivera, and Siqueiros in the United States, 1927--1940.

Ph.D. dissertation, New York University. 2003.

In the late 1920s and continuing through the 1930s the presence of numerous Mexican artists in the United States constituted what has been termed a "Mexican invasion" on the American art scene. In addition to their mural commissions, Diego Rivera, José Clemente Orozco, and David Alfaro Siqueiros created a corpus of portable works (movable mural paintings, easel paintings, and prints) that received critical attention. Portable works with Mexican subject matter by the muralists were shown throughout the United States in group gallery and museum exhibitions that often displayed modern Mexican art alongside pre-Columbian objects as well as folk art, introducing the public to the work of the muralists within the context of a broader commercial interest in ancient artifacts and tourist objects. This dissertation analyzes how the muralists' visions developed and were altered in the context of the United States. I examine various channels by which work by the Mexican muralists became known in the United States, and how it was represented, promoted, and received. This study illuminates how the American reception of portable work produced by the muralists impacted the development of Mexican muralism. The first chapter argues that American reactions to the visualization of the violence of the Mexican Revolution forced Orozco to alter his work in order to accommodate the expectations placed on a Mexican artist and the commercial vicissitudes of the market place. Chapter two proposes that the search for common American cultural origins prompted one of the first blockbuster exhibitions of Mexican art (Mexican Arts which originated at the Metropolitan Museum of Art in 1930) and informed its portrayal of Mexican nationalism. Chapter three considers the critical reception of Rivera's exhibition at The Museum of Modern Art (1931-1932) and argues that the public rejection of the artist's "portable" frescoes indicates that American critics began to reach more informed conclusions about Mexican muralism. An analysis of MoMA's exhibition, Twenty Centuries of Mexican Art (1940), is the focus of the fourth chapter, which reveals Orozco's more successful use of the portable fresco medium and changing attitudes towards Mexican modern art over the course of the decade. [Author Abstract]

6.)   **Lee, A. W.**

Public painting in San Francisco: Diego Rivera and his contemporaries.

Ph.D. dissertation, University of California, Berkeley. 1995.

This dissertation explores the relationship between muralism and radical politics in San Francisco between 1915, the year of the Panama Pacific International Exposition, and 1948, the year in which Anton Refregier completed his cycle of murals for the Rincon Annex Post Office. Its major focus is on three San Francisco murals produced by Diego Rivera, the Mexican artist whose work and very presence brought the city's mural movement into explicit contact with the

Communist Party. The theme which runs through this study is an analysis of muralism's role as public art. For, as it is argued, muralism was not necessarily art for the public, and to claim that it was, as many patrons, painters, and administrators did, required a specific ideological and political climate, a means of bridging art with other, more familiar concerns about the public, and an audience receptive, or at least attentive, to the validity of those claims. Accordingly, the questions which recur in the chapters are several: How were Rivera's works regarded, and how were the debates which surrounded them related to disputes between specific interest groups? How did artists try to map pictorial interests onto political ones, and how did patrons attempt to map political interests onto pictorial ones? What role did debates about the public--in discussions surrounding San Francisco's post-earthquake reconstruction, Progressive politics, labor union agitation, the Popular Front, the New Deal, and the International Expositions--play in permitting patrons and painters to work towards transforming muralism into public art? Most importantly, the dissertation tries to understand the pictorial inventions of the city's muralists--that is, the development of a proper public language--in conjunction with the arguments for and against murals as public art. It traces a mural movement which possessed a certain autonomy and internal consistency, inflected only partially, for example, by larger New Deal programs; and it uncovers the work of numerous local painters who have heretofore been ignored. As such, the dissertation includes detailed reproductions, floorplans, and programs of several mural projects which have not been presented before. [Author Abstract]

7.)   **Mabardi, S. F.**

*Diego   Rivera   between   modernities:
Strategies, negotiations, and shared
categories.*
Ph.D. dissertation, Simon Fraser University
(Canada). 2000.

The Mexican painter and muralist, Diego
Rivera, travelled between centres and
peripheries from 1907 to 1932. My
dissertation examines how the complex
relations between different modernities
mediated Rivera's project to dominate what
Pierre Bourdieu calls the "field of cultural
production" and to effect a shift in artistic
attention from Paris to Mexico and the rest of
North America. I explain Rivera's ultimately

frustrated reception in Europe, his temporary success in the United States, and his dominant role in the construction of a post-revolutionary cultural identity in Mexico. Furthermore, I demonstrate how Rivera's domination of Mexican culture in the twenties, though largely based on his prominent position within muralism, was not limited to painting. He also played an important role in other spheres of cultural production, including literature, Rivera's relationship to the indigenous and popular in Mexico was informed by his earlier experiences with European primitivism(s) from 1907 to 1921, the year he returned to Mexico. He learned the critical stance against bourgeois values and colonialism from

Western primitivism, and the potential for differentiation and identity formation from the use of the popular and indigenous of the Russian primitivists. Rivera's representation of the autochthonous "primitive," both land and people, was an act of affirmation, an attempt at creating a modem, but Mexican, subject and culture. He showed this in his first murals and through his involvement in other cultural areas. In his role as *Mexican Folkways'* art editor and educator, and as poet and "literary character," Rivera played a powerful part in the construction of a Mexican culture in which the indigenous and the popular were an essential component. His association with Mexican avant-garde writers and poets in the 1920s gave him an unusual outlet, and inspired the writer, Xavier Icaza, to make him the main character in a 1926 work about the construction of a postrevolutionary culture and identity. The analysis of this work helps illuminate the contradictions and tensions involved in the elaboration of a cultural identity in the 1920s in a country recovering from the armed phase of the Revolution, and struggling with the impact on Mexican local traditions of a modernity, modernization and modernism from elsewhere. Rivera's dream to extend Mexico's artistic influence to the North became a temporary reality when he was given the opportunity to paint a number of murals in the United States and to show his work at the Museum of Modem Art in

New York in 1931. My analysis of that exhibition uncovers the complex cultural relations of the early thirties between Mexico and the United States, and shows their intellectuals and artists around the oppositions culture/nature, and modem/primitive. My interpretation is from the perspective of both a sociology of art and current Latin American cultural studies. Bourdieu's sociology of art allows for the examination of agency, contingencies, and strategic positioning in the cultural field. In addition, I draw on the theoretical advances of Latin American scholars in anthropology, sociology, art, and literature. These critics stress the need to consider the divergence and convergence between European and

Latin American modernities which enables them to avoid the simplistic and defective analysis of Latin American art and literature as a transplant from Europe. The ways the North (Europe and the United States) and the South (Mexico) construct each other, and respond to each other's construction, help explain the reception of Rivera's work abroad and at home, and Rivera's responses within these relations. [Author Abstract]

8.)   **Maffay, J.**

Diego Rivera and the art of Mexican identity through the lens of existential psychology. Ph.D. dissertation, Ohio University. 2005.

This dissertation explores the artistic contribution of Mexican artist Diego Rivera through his mural cycle in the National Palace in Mexico City dedicated to the history of Mexico. Existential Psychology, in particular the tri-partite construct developed by Viennese psychotherapist Ludwig Binswanger, founder of the Existential School, is used to explain the existential act of identity development both at the micro level through the life of Rivera and, more importantly, at the macro level through the history of Mexico. The work of Binswanger posited that there are three key human relationships that form the nucleus of human identity. First, Umelt and the human relationship to the natural world. Next, Mitwelt and the human relationship to the social world. And finally, Eigenwelt and human relationship to self. These three relationships are used to analyze the monumental murals, dating from 1929 through 1951, found in the National Palace. To this day the mural cycle of Diego Rivera, with its Zapatista/Indianist orientation, continues to influence the Mexico nation. With illiteracy in Mexico during Rivera's time at more than 80%, the visual dialog he established with the Mexican nation has proven very influential to the identity construction of modern Mexico. His interest in Amerindian culture can perhaps best be understood with reference to the profound knowledge and pride that he developed with reference to pre-Conquest Mesoamerican history and art. It was that knowledge and the pride that that Rivera shared with the Mexican nation through his art. [Author Abstract]

9.)   **Manzano, R.**

Beyond an idea in painting.

M.A.L.S. thesis, State University of New York Empire State College. 2005.

The purpose of my studies was to explore multiple meanings of art as a form of communication. My final creative project, "Beyond an Idea in Painting," consisted of a series of transformative paintings depicting multifaceted aspects of society. My research included the work of three artists whose philosophies have an affinity with my own work. They are Pablo Picasso, Diego Rivera and Judy Chicago. Their work aspires to promote the value of art for social change. Social changes bring awareness to people's rights, self-empowerment, and education. In addition to my readings of art history and postmodernism theories, I interacted with professionals in the field, the public, produced and designed exhibitions at the school's gallery, attended lectures, and viewed exhibitions. This exposure taught me a new perspective about art and history in relation to the time, place, circumstances and people involved in the process. [Author Abstract]

10.)   **Markle, W. G.**

Diego Rivera's Portrait of America: Marxism and montage.

Ph.D. dissertation, University of Oregon. 1999.

This study explores the social, political, and artistic context in which Diego Rivera produced the mural cycle Portrait of America for the New Workers School in New York City during the fall of 1933. The New Workers School was the educational arm of the Communist Party Opposition (CPO), an anti-Stalinist communist splinter group. Rivera's mural was composed of 21 fresco panels that depicted the history of class struggle in the United States according to the specific

Marxist position of the CPO. The study demonstrates that Rivera based his compositions on the aesthetic principles of montage which he adopted through his association with members of the Russian avant-garde. The New Workers School murals serve as an arena for a broader discussion of communist politics and Marxist aesthetic principles. They also demonstrate how Rivera's work challenged the conservative tradition of mural painting, restored it to a position of a truly modern public art, and established a new paradigm that framed the production of murals in the United States for the following decades. The argument relies on the visual evidence presented in Rivera's murals before and after he visited the Soviet Union and became associated with Oktyabr (October), a Russian avant-garde artists' association. The group was composed of artists formerly identified with Constructivism whose theory and practice was based on the modern aesthetics of montage and the belief that a revolutionary society demanded a revolutionary art. This practice was in direct conflict with the artistic aims of Socialist Realism, which ultimately became the only accepted form of artistic expression in the Soviet Union under the leadership of Joseph Stalin. The study demonstrates that Rivera's contact with the Oktyabr group transformed his political ideology and artistic theory. These changes are traced through his subsequent work in Mexico and the United States within the context of the cultural conflicts and social turmoil of the 1930s.

[Author Abstract]

11.) **Mitchell, L. A.**

Rivera redefined: A study of the late easel paintings of Diego Rivera.

M.A. thesis, Michigan State University. 1994.

Diego Rivera is one of the best known Mexican artists, and also one of the least known. His lifetime has seen his name make the newspapers countless times, he has made public statements extensively, and hundreds of books have been written about him. Yet, his life is full of complexities, controversies, and contradictions, and, as such, he still escapes us. There has remained around Rivera the air of a hero. While he professed support of a public art, an art that could not be owned by museums or private wealthy homes, he painted throughout his life more than 3,000 easel paintings, and sold many of them to capitalist homes in the United States. Yet, even with the knowledge of his production of many excellent easel printings and their representation in a number of exhibitions, he is somehow still defined exclusively as a muralist to this day. Through an in-depth examination of one of these works and Rivera's artistic and political motives, this thesis attempts to introduce some balance to the definition of the painter. [Author Abstract]

12.)   **Nordholm, H.**

Diego Rivera: Constructing a myth.

A.M. thesis, University of Missouri - Kansas

City. 2011.

Diego Rivera was a master of creating

visual languages to express his ideas and

beliefs. Throughout his life, he actively

sought to define Mexican culture and his life

through his art and his writing. Much of how

he is remembered today: visionary, rebel,

lover; and how Mexico is known to the

world: exotic, colorful, cultural, was carefully

crafted through Rivera's artistic efforts.

Rivera created a visual identity for Mexican

culture by cultivating a mythology for the

nation that in many ways became

synonymous with his own life. He fostered a sense of Mexicanidad, or pride in one's Mexican identity by looking to his country's pre-Columbian heritage as well as its indigenous population and working classes for inspiration. Rivera's work referenced these groups in both style and subject, and in his murals, the ordinary people of Mexico were made extraordinary, modern heroes through the eyes of Diego Rivera. The language he created, however, was meticulously crafted to serve both his artistic and political agendas. Even as he incorporated ancient pre-Columbian imagery into his work, Rivera created a visual and cultural identity for a new, modern Mexico. [Author Abstract]

13.)   **Osorio, E.**

Intersections of architecture, photography, and personhood: Case studies in Mexican modernity.

Ph.D. dissertation, Princeton University.

2006.

This dissertation examines a series of intersections between architecture, photography, and personhood in early to mid-twentieth century Mexico City. By arranging several case studies thematically, by subject, and scale, the dissertation comments on varying forms of expressing and understanding modernity during this period, emphasizing the significance that personal encounters and inscriptions hold in the conceptualization of architecture. It studies temporality and representation as an intersection of privacy and publicity in domesticity and a site to negotiate the tension between the individual and the collective in architecture in which photography provides a lens to observe modernity in post-revolutionary Mexico. Using architect and painter Juan O'Gorman's oeuvre as a point of departure, Chapter One discusses the role of cultural nationalism and the effects of O'Gorman's collaborations with Diego Rivera on the formation of nationally iconic cultural producers. Chapter Two considers the roles of artistic and architectural notions of interiority prominent in Mexico City during the 1930's and '40's, which distinguish themselves from predominant contemporary ideas of exteriority. Chapter Three examines O'Gorman's Mexico City house-studio for Frida Kahlo and Rivera of 1929-32, discussing the house studio, client-architect relationships, the problem of designing a house for a unique couple, the implications for their public and private lives, and the building's analogous relationship to them. Taking a cue from the question of cultural nationalism, Chapter Four examines the photography of Guillermo Kahlo and problematizes the imposition of associations between categories and artists. It explores the representation of architecture, its implications for modernity in the work of a

German-immigrant Mexican photographer whose personal and professional trajectory embodies movement, and its expression of a male gaze. Chapter Five considers the representation of modern architecture in relation to reception in United States publications through the eye of a woman, Esther Born, an American architect-photographer who traveled to Mexico City in the 1930's and actively engaged transnational exchange. Within these locations and their intersecting axes, the dissertation emphasizes the transient, unstable, and reciprocal nature of cultural production that, while looking to the future, is simultaneously caught between the present and past. [Author Abstract]

14.)   **Paquette, C. M.**

Public duties, private interests: Mexican art at New York's Museum of Modern Art, 1929-- 1954.

Ph.D. dissertation, University of California, Santa Barbara. 2002.

MoMA is one of the world's most influential institutions in terms of establishing a canon for modern art. While canons ostensibly connote impartiality, the history of Mexican art at MoMA raises critical questions. Why did MoMA's promotion of Mexican artists vary so dramatically from 1929 to 1954? What forces were in play? I document how MoMA interpreted and evaluated Mexican art during this period, and situate esthetic issues relative to the diverse political and economic pressures brought to bear on MoMA policy. Of special interest are the conceptions of public duty that motivated trustees and staff, and the private interests to which these duties were often related-- especially those of the Rockefeller family. My research draws on publications, reports, correspondence and registration records from MoMA, the Rockefeller Archive Center, Archives of American Art, and the Hoover Institution. While MoMA committed

significant funding to the goal of educating the U.S. and, ultimately, the global public about modern art, the museum also made use of critical discourse for broader purposes. Generally the goal was to promote international understanding and to strengthen U.S.-Mexican or U.S.-Latin American relations. A less publicized aspect of this mission was the promotion of democracy and capitalism and the thwarting of communism in the name of peace and economic progress. Internationalist perspectives coincided with U.S. nationalist and expansionist thinking. The underlying aim in the 1930s, 1940s and 1950s was to attain or maintain the position of the U.S. as global cultural leader--cultural status to match the nation's preeminence in political, financial and military affairs. What was perceived to be in the public interest often was beneficial for the Rockefeller family, including their investments in Latin America.

The museum was adept at manipulating highly varied art styles and trends for ideological purposes. MoMA deployed works by communist artists to promote democratic ideals and the ostensibly free exchange of culture under capitalism. At the same time the museum practiced repressive measures, especially when trustees believed such measures were necessary to safeguard the financial assistance and good will of the institution's supporters. [Author Abstract]

15.)   **Pearson, M. C.**

Diego Rivera's artistic journey.

M.A. thesis, California State University,

Dominguez Hills. 2000.

Diego Rivera likely would not have achieved lasting recognition as an artist if he had not returned from Europe to participate in Mexico's mural program. Using Rivera's autobiography and biographies as well as personal observations of his paintings, the chapters trace his artistic trajectory from his earliest training in Mexico City, to his studies and artwork in Spain and Paris from 1907 to 1921, and to his profound shift in style with fresco painting in Mexico. Reaction to Rivera's work in Europe and his own assessment of it is presented, as well as the immediate and lasting acclaim accorded his murals. The conclusion is that his European work simply followed the European modern art styles of the early twentieth century, without particularly distinguishing him. He developed his own personal style only after returning to Mexico, immersing himself in its culture, and beginning the medium of fresco. [Author Abstract]

16.)   **Picôt, N.**

The representation of the indigenous peoples of Mexico in Diego Rivera's National Palace mural (1929-1935).

Ph.D. dissertation, The University of Nottingham (United Kingdom). 2007.

This thesis is a multidisciplinary project, drawing on the discourses of Visual Cultural Studies, Latin American history and Critical Theory. Insights from each of these disciplines interact to investigate the representation of the indigenous peoples of Mexico in the mural triptych entitled *History of the Mexican People* painted by Diego Rivera in the National Palace, Mexico City, between 1929 and 1935. The main focus is an exploration of the mural as a cultural text, which is formed through socio-political structures and homogenising nationalist visions. The artist is seen as partly a product of history who acts, both consciously and subconsciously, as a conduit for such historical structures. The investigation requires a multi-dimensional approach as it includes emotional, aesthetic, sociological, political, cultural, philosophical, biographical and material elements. A close-reading of the National Palace mural as a cultural `text' is undertaken in order to deconstruct certain culturally-specific political myths. The production of the fresco triptych is inextricably interlinked with the construction of the post-revolutionary Mexican nation and socio-cultural mythologies regarding the `Indian' which are central to nationalist imagery and the post-revolutionary, anthropological theories of *indigenismo*. Certain distinctive racial strands of nationalist mythology which are represented in the mural are analysed within the framework of Anthony D. Smith's (1999) theory of historical ethno-mythology. I argue, following Smith, that what gives nationalism its power are the myths, memories, traditions and symbols of ethnic heritages and the ways in which a popular living past has been, can be and is rediscovered and reinterpreted by modern, nationalist intelligentsias. [Author Abstract]

17.)   **Pozzi-Harris, A. J.**

De-mythologizing Rivera: Political cultures and the European years, 1907-1921.

M.A. thesis, Queen's University (Canada). 1998.

This thesis deals with the period the Mexican artist Diego Rivera spent in Europe (1907-1909; 1911-1921), and with the works produced at that time. Rivera's European production, I propose, can be contextualized within two political cultures: French nationalism during World War I and the post-war era, and the Mexican Revolution. I propose that Rivera's European production accepts a plurality of meanings when contextualized in these distinct political cultures. This dual approach challenges previous readings which have mythologized Rivera's European period as unavoidably linked to the iconography, style, political ideology, and national identity that he manifested after his definitive return to Mexico in 1921. In chapter 2, I contextualize Rivera's transition from Cubism to *la tradition* within the politicized interpretation provided by Kenneth Silver in Esprit de Corps. Between 1913 and early 1917, Rivera was a Cubist artist. Around March 1917, however, he renounced Cubism for a classicized manner of painting, which included Ingres-like portraits, academic drawings, Cezannesque landscapes, and "construction drawings." Relying on Kenneth

Silver's politicized interpretation of the avant-garde shifts between Cubism and *la tradition* during World War I and the early post-war era, I situate Rivera's

confrontational positioning in the midst of the right-wing oriented discourse of French nationalism. This contextualization opens the question as to Rivera's political allegiances in the context of nationalist France. In chapter 3, I analyze Rivera national, cultural, and political allegiances in relation to the Mexican revolution (1910-1921), and I conclude that Rivera's notion of national identity evolved between 1911 and 1921. This evolution, I argue, can be traced through a joint reading of Rivera's representations 'of Mexicans and of Mexico.' Representations of Mexicans encompass Rivera's portraits of Mexican emigres, while representations of Mexico comprise depictions of Mexican *artesania* and of the Mexican plateau. Before 1914 Rivera identified with the liberal, urban, educated class of Mexicans. He manifested this allegiance in two portraits he painted of a representative of this class, culture, and political ideology. Between 1914 and 1919 approximately, Rivera identified with an imagined community of uneducated and violent peasants. Around 1919, however, Rivera's national and cultural identity shifted once again, as he was invited to return to Mexico to collaborate in the "civilizing" of the uneducated Mexicans whom he had previously identified with. Rivera's renewed interest in the 'old masters,' I argue, favorably impressed Mexico's post-revolutionary intellectual elite, who thought his embrace of the classical tradition conducive to their "civilizing mission." In fact, Rivera's classicizing style, Western and Europe-centered as it was, paved the way for his official return to Mexico. [Author Abstract]

18.)   **Rodriguez-Gomez, G.**

Re-Conceptualizing Social Medicine in Diego Rivera's History of Medicine in Mexico: The People's Demand for Better Health Mural, Mexico City, 1953.

M.A. thesis, University of California, Riverside. 2012.

Diego Rivera's History of Medicine in Mexico: The People's Demand for Better Health mural has been interpreted as a representation of the Social Security Institution in Mexico, ancient and modern medicine, or mythological indigenous iconography relative to fecundity. Interestingly, the mural's descriptive title overshadows Rivera's gritty commentary embedded within the depiction of ancient and modern societies of Mexico, specifically Mexico City. The overall narrative chronologically demonstrates a generational shift from the indigenous Nahuatl or Nahua medicine and myth, mainly reproductions of early colonial imagery, to the modern nineteen fifties urban landscape and hospital setting. Highly regarded as a creative interpreter of Mexican tradition and culture, Diego Rivera was not necessarily focused on representing accurate depictions of the ancient societies of Central Mexico. Scholars must reconsider how to approach Rivera's art representing indigenous communities, in this case Nahua mythology and the social need for social security, and analyze their relationship relative to the push for modernity throughout the industrial era. Rivera's artistic vision, coupled with his polemic character, produced a final mural that strongly conveys a multilayered dialogue between the artist, the viewer, and the past. The mural History of Medicine in Mexico: The People's Demand for Better Health actively engages with the viewer through the ongoing regeneration of thoughts, movements, and actions that channel the fluctuations of modernity itself by questioning the institutionalized system and the organic indigenous perspective. Interaction with the mural is necessary to open one's comprehension of not only Rivera's own personal struggle and realizations, but a nations' choice to move forward towards modernization. Ultimately, Rivera's visual articulation of ancient and modern medicine allows the viewer to interact with, exchange ideas and potentially manifest the dynamic yet fragmented essence of an ambiguous modernity. [Author Abstract]

19.) **Younger, J. K.**

Utopia Mexicana: Diego Rivera's program for Chapingo Chapel, 1924--1927.

Ph.D. dissertation, University of Maryland College Park. 1999.

Between 1924 and 1927, Diego Rivera created a mural program for Chapingo chapel, located on the grounds of the Escuela Nacional de Agricultura (ENA) and commissioned by ENA director Marte Gómez and the Minister of Agriculture, Ramón de Negri. After painting several frescoes in the adjacent administration building, Rivera began the chapel murals in the fall of 1924. This space, originally the Catholic chapel of a rural hacienda, was deconsecrated and transformed into the school's formal assembly hall. As a federally sponsored project, Rivera's work at Chapingo, exemplifies the fundamental partnership between art and politics during the Mexican Renaissance. However, as one of the few major mural projects located outside of the Federal District, Chapingo chapel also differs significantly from other murals painted in the capital. Conceived and executed in the aftermath of the Mexican Revolution (1910 1920), Rivera's decoration of Chapingo chapel must be considered in the context of postrevolutionary state-building. Rivera's painted walls engage important social and political issues of the day, and contribute to contemporary discourse concerning the future of the Mexican nation. The chapel murals project and reflect revolutionary ideology regarding race, gender, eugenics, anti-clericalism, Communism and agrarian reform. This dissertation examines the nexus of these ideas as they converge within the context of the chapel space. By approaching the chapel program through its historical context, I understand the space as a cultural artifact that lends valuable insight into the early years of postrevolutionary reconstruction. Theorizing both the production and reception of the chapel program, I address broader questions concerning the federal patronage of mural painting, the construction of national community, and the importance of modernity as aesthetic strategy, cultural policy and political platform. [Author Abstract]

Locating Dissertations and Theses

A. Purchase

Many of the dissertations and theses listed in this bibliography are available for purchase through UMI Dissertation Express:

http://disexpress.umi.com/dxweb

By Fax:

800-864-0019

By Mail:

789 E. Eisenhower Parkway, P.O. Box 1346, Ann Arbor, Michigan 48106-1346

800-521-3042

B. Interlibrary Loan

Dissertations and theses may also be requested through Interlibrary Loan via your local public, college or university library.

www.ingramcontent.com/pod-product-compliance
Lightning Source LLC
Chambersburg PA
CBHW070846180526
45168CB00002B/973